This short look at the principles and practice of Puritan diary-keeping will surely inspire a resurgence of this spiritual discipline in today's church, and not before time. Dr Birkett makes an excellent case for the benefits it brings to individuals and to the wider church.

Dr Ros Clarke, Associate Director, Church Society

St Antholin's Lecture 2021

SPIRITUAL PRACTICES OF THE PURITANS:

THE IMPORTANCE OF DIARY-KEEPING

KIRSTEN BIRKETT

The Latimer Trust

The Latimer Trust (formerly Latimer House, Oxford) is a conservative Evangelical research organisation within the Church of England, whose main aim is to promote the history and theology of Anglicanism as understood by those in the Reformed tradition. Interested readers are welcome to consult its website for further details of its many activities.

The Latimer Trust
London N14 4PS UK
Registered Charity: 1084337
Company Number: 4104465
Web: www.latimertrust.org
E-mail: administrator@latimertrust.org

CONTENTS

Introduction

The Puritans are rightly famous for their efforts to maintain godliness of life. They emphasised the importance of habit; what is practiced habitually will have an effect on action and character. The point was not to have mere outward conformity, but a changed inner life, including inner movement towards God in motivation and emotion, and the increase of joy in God's blessings. Part of the habit of life that was recommended, and practised, by many Puritans, was diary-keeping; a regular, written account of life, in which events could be noted and godly reactions practised. This was to be a method of putting one's mind to godly use, reflecting on the events of life and their import for the kingdom of God, and reflection upon one's inner life in an attempt to be both accountable, and to encourage personal growth towards God. No part of life was considered exempt from the ongoing effort to grow in godliness, and writing an account of that life could both record and encourage that growth.

Such diary-writing could be seen as an almost morbid introspection. However scholars have agreed that that would be to misunderstand the purpose of Puritan diarising. As William Haller wrote, 'the seeming morbidity of many [Puritans of the] time was merely that of a hard-working idealist momentarily overwrought but the next moment recovering from his lassitude to be again energetic, eloquent and courageous according to his lights'.[1] The Puritans wrote precisely because they wished to avoid morbidity; instead of giving way to ungodly thoughts or emotions, they wrote themselves into a better state of mind.

> The diary like the autobiography, of which it was the forerunner, was the Puritan's confessional. In its pages he could fling upon his God the fear and weakness he found in his heart but would not betray to the world. [A Puritan] therefore, must not be set down too promptly as a morbid introvert, aesthetically insensitive, intellectually incurious, abnormally moralistic. His diary is enough to show that such is far from being the whole truth. It was obviously written as a religious exercise and for psychological relief by a man who had to be continually snatching for time in which to do the things he most wanted to accomplish.[2]

The diary-writing of the Puritans was to become a genre of self-examination, that would grow throughout the

[1] William Haller, *The Rise of Puritanism, or, the way to the New Jerusalem as set forth in pulpit and press from Thomas Cartwright to John Lilburne and John Milton, 1570–1643* (New York and London: Columbia University Press, 1938), 39.

[2] Haller, *Rise of Puritanism*, 38. Haller's example here is Richard Rogers, whom we will be considering later in this paper. See also Owen Watkins, *The Puritan Experience: Studies in Spiritual Autobiography* (New York: Schocken, 1972).

seventeenth century and become a literary movement in its own right. Samuel Pepys's diaries, Richard Baxter's writings on spiritual experiences, and even John Bunyan's *Grace Abounding* could be seen in this tradition.[3] Puritan self-writing was 'an exercise in emotional health and religious testimony, taking daily events and sorrowful realities and, through the process of writing, turning them into sanctified, if momentary, present emotional experiences'.[4]

John Beadle: Diary-writing in Theory

The theory of Puritan diary-writing was set out by John Beadle, well into the period when diary-writing was becoming popular.[5] Beadle based his work on Numbers 33:2: 'And Moses wrote their goings out, according to their Journeys, by the commandment of the Lord.' He thought this reason for all Christians to keep diaries: '... they had a Journal of all Gods mercies, and why not we a Diary of all Gods gracious dealings with us?'[6] Holding a high view of the value of writing in general, he took this example of Moses' record-keeping to recommend that Christian believers keep records of their own lives.

---

[3] James S. Lambert, '"Raised unto a cheareful and lively belleeving": the 1587–90 diary of the Puritan Richard Rogers and writing into joy,' *Studies in Philology* (2016): 254–81.

[4] Lambert, 'Raised,' 254.

[5] John Beadle, *The Journal or Diary of a Thankful Christian: Presented in some meditations upon Numb. 33.2* (London, 1656).

[6] Beadle, *Journal*, 13.

The main problem of Christian life, as Beadle saw it, was forgetfulness; and this is a terrible sin, common to most people.

> Such is the corruption of all, even the best men by nature, that though in their adversity they seek God early, yet in their prosperity they forget him commonly. They, that in a dark evening are glad of a little star-light, in the day are scarce thankful for the Sun ... It is a most provoking sin to forget God, and the great mercies he hath bestowed on them.[7]

Luther, indeed, had written that there were three things in particular for Christians to watch for, as destructive of Christianity: 'carnal security, worldly policy, and forgetfulness of God's benefits.'[8]

God gave the Israelites ceremonies and practices in order to remember him. Jesus, similarly, instituted the Lord's Supper, to be performed in remembrance of him. God provided Scripture, inspiring the biblical writers to record his deeds so that future generations would know of them. It is vitally important for God's people to remember; this has the double purpose of inspiring thankfulness, and warning of evil. 'To keep a Journall or Diary by us', Beadle

---

[7] Beadle, *Journal*, 1–2.

[8] Beadle, *Journal*, 5.

concludes, 'especially of all Gods gracious dealings with us, is a work for a Christian of singular use.'[9]

This was to be a diary of records; but, more particularly, of 'the mercies that have been bestowed on us',[10] following the examples of Moses and David. The diary should have entries of two types. Christians should first record national and public things, then private and personal things.

Public matters

Beadle's suggestions for the public matters that the Christian ought to record were extensive.

1. 'Take notice what Kings and Princes, what Magistrates and Governors have ruled over us; for commonly, Such Prince, such people'.[11] Rulers influence the people; the Christian should, therefore, know the character of the current ruling figures.

2. 'Observe what that Religion is, that by those Magistrates is imbraced, and how the truth is countenanced or opposed by them'.[12] The best way to govern is based on true religion; far from being a private issue, or one of indifference, it matters what religious beliefs a ruler has.

---

[9] Beadle, *Journal*, 10.

[10] Beadle, *Journal*, 11.

[11] Beadle, *Journal*, 14.

[12] Beadle, *Journal*, 16.

3. 'Keep an account of the various and changeable condition of the Times in the Countrey where we live, either for prosperity or adversity, with the fruits and effects of both'.[13] This is simply a matter of staying abreast of what is happening in one's country.

4. 'Keep a Diary of the several and most remarkable judgements that God hath in our time inflicted upon notorious offenders, whether persons in high places, or such as moved in a lower orbe'.[14] It is noticeable that Beadle emphasises *God's* judgement of offenders; the Christian is never to forget God's sovereignty and interest in daily matters.

5. 'Finally, consider seriously, and observe very strictly, what the Nationall Epidemicall sin of the time and present generation may be'.[15] Such sin should be noticed, and analysed; it is all too easy to take for granted, or to brush over, what is familiar.

This is worth reflection upon. We twenty-first century Christians are, perhaps, so used to non-Christian government that we rarely keep watch in these terms. Now, however, we have far more power to influence government, in our days of representative democracy, than did most people in Beadle's day. We should be aware of what is going on, not to make ourselves depressed but to show a proper care – and to pray.

---

[13] Beadle, *Journal*, 19.

[14] Beadle, *Journal*, 22.

[15] Beadle, *Journal*, 25.

Private matters

That is what we should be noting in the public sphere. Then Beadle goes on, write about your own life, present and past. In fact, we should all write about our own conversion. 'Let every man keep a strict account of his effectuall calling, and of his age in Christ; and (if it may be) set down the time when, the place where, and the person by whom he was converted'.[16] After all, in Beadle's reasoning, this is the most wonderful thing you can write about; the miracle that every Christian can testify to. '... it is not only matter of wonder now, but will be cause of admiration unto all eternity!'[17] For the present, take note of blessings, and instances of God's help. This will help us to see that all we have is from God. 'Take special notice of all divine assistance, and that either in the performance of the duties that are required of us, or in bearing those evils that are inflicted upon us'.[18] Again, this reminds us of God's constant sovereign care, which we may not notice if we do not pay special attention, and record it; this is necessary to ensure our thankfulness.

> Remember, and for that end put into your Journal all deliverances from dangers, vouchsafed to you or yours. And indeed, what is our whole life, but a continued deliverance?[19]

[16] Beadle, *Journal*, 48.

[17] Beadle, *Journal*, 51.

[18] Beadle, *Journal*, 51.

[19] Beadle, *Journal*, 55.

This is reminiscent of the Pentecost Collect from the Book of Common Prayer: 'Grant us by the same Spirit to have a right judgment in all things, and evermore to rejoice in his holy comfort'. This is an apt prayer: do we daily rejoice and thank God, for the ever-present gift of the Holy Spirit and his comfort? What difference would it make to our lives if we did?

Beadle goes on with more specific things to write about, and to be thankful for. We are to give thanks for 'All the instruments, all the men and means that God hath in providence at any time used for our good'[20] – such as godly parents, schoolteachers, ministers and so on. 'And finally, mark ... what answers God gives to your prayers' because these are 'remarkable pledges of his love'.[21] In other words, 'Labour by faith to see and observe God in all things that are bestowed on you'[22] – things such as health, peace, liberty, rain, or goods. Through such means, 'By the eye of faith behold the wisdom, goodnesse, and power of God in his works, though he be invisible'.[23]

God will keep his promises, Beadle reminds us, so keep a record of how he does so. We should remind ourselves of how his promises to us have been fulfilled through Christ, and perhaps also through other people. As we write of this, Beadle instructs, we should observe God's wisdom and goodness in the means he chooses. God will

---

[20] Beadle, *Journal*, 58.

[21] Beadle, *Journal*, 62.

[22] Beadle, *Journal*, 66.

[23] Beadle, *Journal*, 68.

Do we daily rejoice and thank God, for the ever-present gift of the Holy Spirit and his comfort?

What difference would it make to our lives if we did?

choose the right time to answer our prayers. Notice what he gives, and that he has not given more. If he saw us fit to use more, he could and would give more. It is a mercy for our minds to be conformable to our means. Be content. God can give things if he thinks them good for us.

The diary was not to be written, then stashed away on a shelf. There are records of Puritan diaries being circulated amongst congregations as examples and encouragements.[24] Beadle, for his part, urges the individual to read his own diary, to remember all the recorded blessings, which was the original purpose of writing it. We are to remember just how much God has given us. We are to remember how great our need is, in our sinfulness. Remembering these things gives us a right humbleness. It is good to remember what God gives us, and how he might supply our needs in other ways that we did not think of. Richard Baxter similarly suggested that the Christian write down what the 'heart perceive' in a 'diary or book of Heart accounts', for this alters the reader, to become more hopeful. What was written was to be read later; 'The diary should act as a book of accounts, depositing feelings in order to withdraw them at a more needful time'.[25]

Beadle especially urges us to take note of answered prayers, or blessings, that come in ways we did not expect. If we

---

[24] Andrew Cambers, 'Reading, the godly, and self-writing in England, circa 1580–1720,' *Journal of British Studies* 46 (2007): 813.
[25] Lambert, 'Raised,' 261.

do not have what we desire, he encourages us to muse, well, what else *do* we have? Adam, for example, could not eat the one fruit, but could eat every other. Moses could not go into Canaan, yet he had an honourable burial. God gives generously; we should remember that, not let the want of some desired thing destroy thankfulness and joy in the many other blessings.

At the same time, we are to 'Reckon often, not onely what you have and what you want, but what you may want'.[26] That is, we should remain aware of the fragility of the world. We can ask God for anything: in fact, that is precisely what we should do in prayer, rather than worry about it. However, we can leave the dispensing to God. He knows the best way to do it.

While being thankful for worldly blessings, we should also take the opportunity to remember that the things of this world are passing away. We naturally desire empty things; we should remind ourselves of the 'vanity of all creature-comforts, honours, pleasures, riches, friends'.[27] They are not to be loved out of proportion. They must not be made idols of. Covetousness is an evil sin, making us ungrateful for what we have, and robbing us of joy.

Also, Beadle exhorts us, we are not to rely excessively upon other people, even though God does provide much good to us through others. They are not responsible for

---

[26] Beadle, *Journal*, 115.
[27] Beadle, *Journal*, 118.

our joy. 'Have communion with few; be intimate with one; deal justly with all; speak evill of none'.[28]

In such ways we can benefit from the keeping of a diary. Having written, and read, we may ask ourselves three questions. First, 'What honour do I bring to God for all this?'[29] That is, are we praising God sufficiently and living for him? Second, 'What good do I do to my neighbour?'[30] If God has been generous to us, how are we responding in generosity to others? Finally, ask 'what good you yourselves get by all that God hath done for you'.[31] In other words, am I making the most of all this health, and wealth, and good days? This gospel and this peace? Do I grow? This is a major emphasis of Puritan writings. We are here to prepare for the next life. Our job here is to grow in Christlikeness. That is how to judge what do to with any opportunity.

Being thankful

It is not enough simply to write of our lives and thoughts. We do so in order to be thankful. That is precisely why we keep a diary. Especially, Beadle urges, be thankful for Jesus and the unsearchable riches of God's grace in him; be thankful for afflictions, which are also instances of God's grace; bless God for every day he has kept you from scandal and sin; and bless God not just for what you

---

[28] Beadle, *Journal*, 127.

[29] Beadle, *Journal*, 112.

[30] Beadle, *Journal*, 131.

[31] Beadle, *Journal*, 137.

have, and what you want, but also what you hope to have. There is more to come; we shall enter into joy.

Thankfulness can become a habit, a way of life. It can spill over into other relationships. So, we do not merely ask our friends to pray for us; we ask them to thank God with us.

Too few Christians, Beadle says in conclusion, keep a diary 'of all Gods gracious dealings with them'.[32] Yet we have been told so forcefully in Scripture that God wants us to remember. 'It is good therefore not only to remember our low and sinful estate, that we may be humble, but to understand the loving kindness of the Lord, that we may record his favours'.[33] Understanding comes from attention, reflection and study; writing about these things is part of such tasks.

In my Christian life, having sat under many, many sermons, I have never yet been urged to keep a diary as part of Christian duty. It appears to be a spiritual discipline that has, in this country at least, fallen out of prominence. Yet Beadle, and other Puritans, saw this as a vital part of living as a Christian. All should be keeping a record of God's activities in the world and in our lives; what is happening, how and when. For Beadle, this was simply obvious, a basic truth. Moreover, he points out cheerfully, your memory is bad and will only get worse. Forgetting God is a sin, that leads to many other sins.

---

[32] Beadle, *Journal*, 152.

[33] Beadle, *Journal*, 156.

God is rightly angry at our forgetting: so we must take action to help ourselves remember.

Christian biographies

Another point that Beadle makes, which similarly is less frequent in modern Christian life, is that keeping a diary will help your friends when they write a history of your life. That point in itself may well make us reflect on whether we should remember better the lives of our fellows. Better than reading the biography of some celebrity, why do we not produce the edifying biographies of faithful Christians? Their everyday struggles, their efforts to grow in godliness, God's work in their lives?

Keeping a diary, Beadle says, brings Christians into closer knowledge of God and his nature. It makes us better love our Lord, better love our neighbour, and brings us to humility as we recognise God's kindness. Over all this, it brings us to thankfulness. Diary-keeping, in his eyes, is simply part of enlarging our faith.

Such was the theory; and the practices it recommended were, one might think, too onerous for any individual to keep. Yet the practice of Puritan diary-keeping was, as we have seen, highly popular and a growing genre by the time of Beadle's work. The foundational example, perhaps lying behind Beadle's exhortations, is the diary of the Puritan Richard Rogers.

Keeping a diary brings
Christians into closer
knowledge of God and
his nature.

It makes us better love
our Lord, better love
our neighbour, and
brings us to humility
as we recognise
God's kindness.

Richard Rogers: Diary-writing in Practice

Rogers was one of the writers recommended by Richard Baxter as 'affectionate and practical': practical 'because they taught men what to believe and how to act', affectionate 'because they appealed through the imagination to men's emotions'.[34] They wanted to make 'every man see himself under the eternal images of the pilgrim and the warrior'.[35] Rogers' diary shows a life of pastoral ministry, in which he studied Scripture, wrote sermons, visited, prayed, and worked not just to do more godly things but to bring about a godly state of mind in which he rejoiced in the things of God. Rogers thought the greatest danger, even in a dangerous life, was fear; this must be faced, for it was the work of the devil.

> The preacher kept a diary not as a diversion but as a tactical manoeuvre against the adversary within. He could get the better of discouragement and nervous depression by thus driving his black moods out into the forefront of consciousness. Satan grew powerless when looked squarely in the eye.[36]

Rogers wrote of eight duties of the Christian, to be practiced every day.

---

[34] Haller, *Rise of Puritanism*, 25. Baxter inherited Rogers' journals and referred to them in his own writings. Lambert, 'Raised,' 256, note 20.

[35] Haller, *Rise of Puritanism*, 25.

[36] Haller, *Rise of Puritanism*, 41.

First, that euerie[37] day wee should be humbled for our sins as through due examination of our lives by the law of God we shall see them.

That euerie day we be raised up in assured hope of the forgiueness of them by the promises of God in Christ.

That euery day we prepare our hearts to seek the Lord still, and keep them fit and willing thereto.

That euery day we strongly, and resolutely are our selues against all euill and sinne, ferrying[38] most of all to offend God.

That euery day we nourish and fear and loue of him, and ioy in him more than in any thing, and indeuour to please him in all duties as occasions shall be offered, looking for him coming. 2 Thes. 3.5.

That euery day our thanks be continued for benefits received, and still certainly hoped for.

That euerie day we watch and pray for steadfastnesses and Constance in all these.

---

[37] every (here and following); 'u' was often used in place of 'v'.
[38] fearing

That euerie day wee hold and keep our peace with God, and so lie down with it.

And this is the direction which euerie Christian must practise euerie day in his life, and these are the necessarie parts of it, which may not be omitted any day at all without sinne; nor carelesly and wittingly without great sin.[39]

The *Seven Treatises*,[40] a book on Christian life which Rogers thought of as a result of his own diary-keeping,[41] recorded at length the daily habits 'to be observed for the effecting of a godly life', most of them concerning state of mind. It is not just a matter of deeds, Rogers wrote; 'our conversation should be in heaven, that is, that our common course of this life should be heavenlie'.[42] This required, among other things, watchfulness and meditation; private habits of thought and action to promote godliness. Watchfulness is 'a carefull observing of our hearts, and diligent looking to our ways, that they may be pleasing, and acceptable unto God';[43] meditation, to go with it, is a 'spiritual exercise ... which putteth life

---

[39] Richard Rogers, Samuel Ward and M M Knappen, *Two Elizabethan Puritan Diaries* (Delhi, Facsimile Publishers, 2018), 7.

[40] Richard Rogers, *Seven Treatises: containing directions, out of Scripture, leading to true happiness* (London, 1610).

[41] Lambert, 'Raised,' 261, n. 20

[42] Rogers, *Seven Treatises*, 203.

[43] Rogers, *Seven Treatises*, 300.

and strength into all other duties, and parts of Gods worship'.[44] Meditation may be

> ... of any part of Gods word; of God himself, his wisdom, power, his mercie; of the infinite varieties of good things which wee receive of his free bountie; also of his works and judgements; or on our estate, as our sinnes, and the vilenesse of our corruption, that wee yet carry about us; or of our moralities; of the changes in this world, of our deliverance from sinne, and death; of the manifold afflictions of this life, and how wee may in best manner beare and goe throw them, and the benefit thereof, and the ... great privileges which wee enjoy daily, through the immeasurable kindnesse of God towards us; but specially of those things which we have most special need of.[45]

Rogers' diary is a record of just these sorts of endeavours. His diary was part of his effort to instil these habits in himself. In the diary, he humbled himself, wrote of his hope, wrote of God and blessings, and talked himself into a more godly state of mind when he was depressed by his sin. His diary reminded himself of his resolutions, gave him the opportunity to examine himself and his recent actions and so correct himself if needed, and the

---

[44] Rogers, *Seven Treatises*, 312.

[45] Rogers, *Seven Treatises*, 312.

means to make a new resolution to improve. He recorded meetings with other Christians, and the joy he had in sharing gospel truths with them, and so relived that joy in writing about it. The encouragement his companions gave him in godliness was reinforced by keeping a record of it.

The diary is overtly, and deliberately, emotional. Rogers did not just write of his thoughts, but of his emotions as he had them. He recorded emotions as a way of understanding his frame of mind and godliness. He would write to give his emotions a more godly focus, and bring himself to joy and comfort in reminding himself of the gospel. Rogers wrote frequently of emotional pleasure as his goal. This was fairly typical of Puritans; they sought, and experienced, great joy. They expected, and practiced, that it was entirely right to rejoice in God and his blessings. Rogers wanted to make godliness his delight, and, it seems, frequently achieved it.

It was not joy and contentment from having an easy life. Most Puritans lived through very turbulent times and could fear persecution. One of Rogers' diary entries wrote of 'fearful noise of war and trouble in our land', such as attacks from Spain. Rogers also experienced considerable loss because of his insistence on biblical truth. Death was a constant; Rogers' first wife died, and he records the death of several friends. Yet he put all his experiences in the perspective of Scripture. He wrote after the death of one friend:

He wrote to give his emotions a more godly focus, and bring himself to joy and comfort in reminding himself of the gospel.

The Puritans sought, and experienced, great joy.

And I pray God I may joy less in the world
for this cause. I have firmly purposed to
make my whole life a meditation of a
better life, and godliness in every part,
even my occupation and trade, that I may
from point to point and from step to step
with more watchfulness walk with the
Lord. Oh, the infinite gain of it.[46]

Rogers did not write daily. Sometimes his entries
summarised a whole month. He would record events,
then reflect upon them: things happening around
him, events in his ministry, small interactions with
individuals, larger meetings, and always what was going
on in his heart, that he reviewed and tried to make more
godly. He might begin with despair over sin, then turn it
into joy over God's mercy. Events were often the prompt
of an entry, but reflection, often emotional reflection, was
always part.

My heart hath been much occupied in
thinking of the uncertainty of our life
and the momentary brittleness of things
below by occasion of the death of Mr
Leaper [a local minister]. I find my self at
great liberty by this means, when I find a
sensible contempt of this world and joyful
expectation of departure from hence.[47]

---

[46] Rogers, Ward and Knappen, *Two Elizabethan Puritan Diaries*, 64.
[47] Rogers, Ward and Knappen, *Two Elizabethan Puritan Diaries*, 53–54.

Rogers would reflect on his growth in godliness, both in the short term, and in comparison with earlier times in his life.

> Thus I have set down some part of those things which have fallen out this month and the sweet peace which I find and feel since I wrote this, which seasons my heart with aptness and willingness to do duty aright, differs unspeakably from that untowardness which before was in me. For in this state my mind is on some good thing with delight and upon transitory things which little regarding them. But before it was my chiefest delight to be thinking upon any profit or vain pleasure, even long before I had to do with them.[48]

Sometimes, an entry would mostly bewail his own sinfulness and lack of joy.

> August 4, 1587: I cannot yet settle myself to my study [of the Bible], but through unfitness of mind, weakness of body, and partly discontinuing of diligence thereat am held back, and in every kind of it so behind hand, more than some years agone, that I am much discouraged.[49]

---

[48] Rogers, Ward and Knappen, *Two Elizabethan Puritan Diaries*, 54.

[49] Rogers, Ward and Knappen, *Two Elizabethan Puritan Diaries*, 56.

Yet even the middle of winter could be a time of encouragement.

> Nov 29, 1587: Since my last writing God continued his kindness to me, for I have had a comfortable and sensible feeling of the contempt of the world and in study, good company, and other peaceable thinking of the liberty and happiness in christianity so occupied that I have not meanly thought of earthly peace or provision, neither of any increasing of our commodities, although godes hand is not shortened to us that way. I thank god ... I have not had so continual fitness and cheerfulness of mind to such duties as lay upon me in any manner as here of late. And this is the benefit of keeping rule over my mind and bridling my rebellious heart, that whereas in the untowardness of it, all things taken in hand go forward untowardly and there is an unwillingness to holy exercises, yet by mastering it the time in other things was with much cheerfulness and fruit bestowed.[50]

After one particular meeting:

> In my return home my mind by the way was taken up in very heavenly sort,

---

[50] Rogers, Ward and Knappen, *Two Elizabethan Puritan Diaries*, 65.

> rejoicing not a little that the lord had
> so enlarged my heart as that my old
> and accustomed dreams and fantasies
> of things below were vanished and
> drowned. The meditations of my heart
> were such as carried me to the Lord, and
> full graciously seasoned me against my
> coming home.[51]

Overall, Rogers' goal was a constant state of mind and heart that kept God foremost. Rogers often records his feelings fluctuating. It can sound obsessive, and can sound as if he is obsessed with sin in particular; one can see why commentators might think Puritans were overly concerned with sin.[52] However, what he does is understandable: those of us who have experienced joy in God and in godliness, which is so hard to obtain because we are sinful, know the importance of such an experience. Rogers evidently talked to his friends about this, too:

> After our meeting according to our
> custom this 30 of November I had a
> very sweet conference with Mr L. of the
> practice of godliness, of the necessary
> fruit and comfort of it, of the way to

---

[51] Rogers, Ward and Knappen, *Two Elizabethan Puritan Diaries*, 67.

[52] John Stachniewski, for instance, wrote of the despair of the Calvinist Puritan (*The Persecutory Imagination: English Puritanism and the Literature of Despair* (New York: Oxford University Press, 1991)); Lambert argues, however, that Stachniewski fails to notice the way in which Puritans constantly undertook practices to correct any hint of despair. Lambert, 'Raised,' 258.

> bring it forth ... After, at night, we had a
> meeting, a bethinking of ourselves how
> we might rouse up ourselves to a father
> care of beseeming the gospel, which
> was very fruitful. After this also I was in
> comfortable plight, feeling no hindrance
> from having my heart upon the Lord.[53]

Rogers' emotions were very important to him, not just because he wanted what Scripture commanded – joy in God – but also because it was such a strong motivator for him to godly action. And so, he wrote about it, precisely because this practice was a beneficial way to move himself into a more godly frame of mind, which was not just more enjoyable, but would also spur him on to further godliness.

Conclusion: How to Deal with Hardship

We conclude with eleven reasons Rogers gave himself for rejoicing, when he was under threat of being suspended from ministry because of his Puritan principles. It is an excellent example of the way in which writing encouragement can truly be a discipline of godliness and joy; a way of talking oneself into the perspective that God would have us have.

> Nov 3 1589: It is one of the greatest crosses
> which could have befallen me, so I saw it
> very necessary to stay up my weakness

---

[53] Rogers, Ward and Knappen, *Two Elizabethan Puritan Diaries*, 68–69.

with some strength of persuasions to rest contented and thankful to God under it, and prepared with fit readiness and cheerfulness to any good which my place may yield. As first this was one:

1. Seeing it is of the Lord, his will, and thus good reason it should be mine.

2. Seeing I have enjoyed comfortable liberty so long.

3. Seeing I did not honour God in studying for my sermons as sometime, and as I should have done.

4. Seeing it is the lot of my betters, yea and a heavier portion than this also, as deprivation of living, imprisonment.

5. Seeing my beginning how unlike I was, not only not to govern myself, but much less a part of God's church. I have no cause to take it hardly.

6. Seeing the iniquity of the time affords no better thing, but grows to hinder and cut down those means which are seen to stop the cause of sin most.

7. Seeing God, by this, means to rouse me from making this world my heaven, which, as I am like enough to

offend in and go maying in respect of my corruption, so the rather for that many good men are deceived with it.

8. Seeing the Lord will exercise my faith, patience, obedience etc hereby.

9. Seeing he will prepare me for greater afflictions by this.

10. Seeing he would keep me from further corruption of the time, which might, by little and little, winning ground in me, blindfold my judgement and weaken that little measure of good conscience, godly zeal, and courage for the glory of God, which is in me, wherein I pray God that our coldness, in giving place to all that is thrust upon us, be not laid to our charge, while none stand up against it.

11. Seeing the Lord leaves many encouragements to me, in respect of many other, both in the people's love, and in communion with them, and otherwise.

12. Seeing I suffer not, though the reproach and grief and discommodity be great, not as an evil doer, but for

the quietness of my conscience,
1 Peter 3.[54]

Rogers strived to make his reactions godly. He did this by reminding himself of godly reasons to see a situation in a better light, and by writing himself into a better state of mind. We can learn from his example.

---

[54] Rogers, Ward and Knappen, *Two Elizabethan Puritan Diaries*, 91.

Previous St. Antholin Lectures

2001–2010

Peter Adam	Word and Spirit: The Puritan-Quaker Debate
Wallace Benn	Usher on Bishops: A Reforming Ecclesiology
Peter Ackroyd	Strangers to Correction: Christian Discipline and the English Reformation
David Field	"Decalogue" Dod and his Seventeenth Century Bestsellers: A 400th Anniversary Appreciation
Chad B Van Dixhoorn	A Puritan Theology of Preaching
Peter Adam	'To Bring Men to Heaven by Preaching': John Donne's Evangelistic Sermons
Tony Baker	1807–2007 John Newton and the Twenty-First Century
Lee Gatiss	From Life's First Cry: John Owen on Infant Baptism and Infant Salvation
Andrew Atherstone	Evangelical Mission and Anglican Church Order: Charles Simeon Reconsidered
David Holloway	Re-establishing the Christian Faith - and the Public Theology Deficit

Lectures from 2001–2010 are compiled in *Preachers, Pastors, and Ambassadors: Puritan Wisdom for Today's Church*. Edited by Lee Gatiss.

1991–2000

Lectures from 1991–2000 are compiled in *Pilgrims, Warriors, and Servants: Puritan Wisdom for Today's Church*. Edited by Lee Gatiss.

Other books in this series:

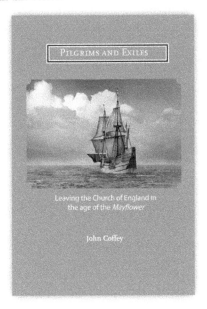

2020 was the 400th anniversary of the sailing of the Mayflower across the Atlantic. Both the voyage of the Mayflower in 1620 and the so-called 'First Thanksgiving' of 1621 would be incorporated into the creation myth of modern America. The transatlantic migration of the Pilgrims was the result of another spiritual migration – before they left Europe, they had left the Church of England. Persecuted in the East Midlands, the Separatists had fled to the Protestant Netherlands for refuge, before sailing for America. In the reign of James I, this made them an oddity, but over the next two generations, hundreds of thousands of others would make this spiritual pilgrimage too.

Professor John Coffey looks at what motivated the Pilgrims and exiles of 1620 at a time when leaving the Church of England was quite exceptional even for Puritans.

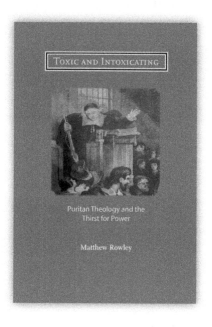

TOXIC AND INTOXICATING

Puritan Theology and the
Thirst for Power

Matthew Rowley

The thirst for power changed Puritan theology, often in ways
that went unnoticed. The rise and decline of political puritanism
afforded unique theological temptations. As victors or victims,
many approached cultural conflict with a deep sense their cause was
righteous — and this often blinded them to the ways they victimised
others. This lecture focuses on the darker moments of Puritan history
and explains how some of their worst actions flowed from good
intentions and admirable qualities. I explore nine ways their theology
staggered under the influence of politics. We must remember this
history and learn from it if we are to avoid toxic and intoxicating
mixtures of piety and patriotism!

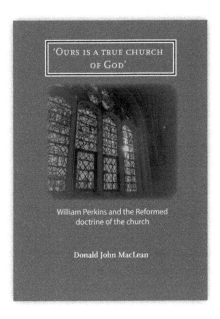

How do we discern a "true" church? Given the current ecclesiastical
climate this is an increasingly pressing question. This study looks at
how William Perkins, a great seventeenth-century Church of England
theologian, responded to this issue.

Particular focus is given to his understanding of the distinctions
between the visible and invisible church, and the marks of a "true"
church, namely, word, sacraments and discipline. Judged against
these marks, Perkins argued passionately that the Church of England
was "a true church of God". Perkins' careful teaching calls us to
consider our response to declension in the church today. Ultimately
his ecclesiology calls us to have a high view of the unity of the visible
church, and in many causes to labour for recovery rather than to leave.

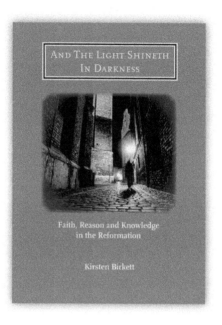

And The Light Shineth In Darkness

Faith, Reason and Knowledge
in the Reformation

Kirsten Birkett

The Bible describes a fallen world and fallen humanity, in which minds are darkened. We reject God and suppress the truth about him. How, then, can we know him at all? In other words, what are the noetic effects of sin? During the Reformation, doctrines of total depravity and the effects of the fall on the whole person re-emerged, with consequent implications for epistemology. If minds are fallen, how can we expect to know anything accurately? The purpose of this study is to start to answer that question by looking at some of the epistemology we find emerging from the writings of John Calvin and Martin Luther.

Other book recommendations:

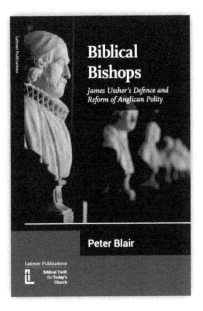

Are bishops biblical?

As fissures emerge within the worldwide Anglican communion, the principle and praxis of episcopacy have never been more pertinent. For some Anglicans, bishops are essential for the church. For others, they are something of a necessary evil; baggage from the English reformation that we might be better off without.

These concerns are nothing new. In the seventeenth century, debates surrounding the validity and authority of bishops abounded. Into those debates wrote James Ussher, archbishop of Armagh and Primate of All Ireland. Ussher was a remarkable figure: a preeminent historian, biblical scholar, and theologian, respected by English puritans and

Irish Jesuits alike. As is often the case with such luminaries, various camps have claimed Ussher as their own; whether they be puritan, high church, or anglo-catholic.

By studying Ussher's ecclesiastical career and his two works on church government, this study assesses Ussher's episcopalian convictions, particularly regarding the validity and authority of bishops. In doing so, it hopes to reintroduce Ussher to the evangelical Anglican world, and demonstrate that episcopacy is not a necessary evil, but a force for good in the church of God.

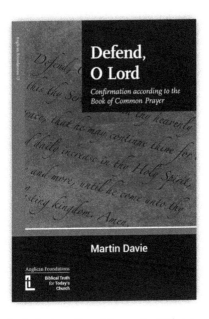

Defend,
O Lord

Confirmation according to the
Book of Common Prayer

Martin Davie

Anglican Foundations
Biblical Truth
for Today's
Church

A key way in which the benefits of the work of Christ are conveyed to those who respond to the gospel with repentance and faith is through the two rites of 'Christian initiation': baptism and confirmation. In baptism we die to our old life of sin and death and rise to a new life with God which will be fully revealed at the resurrection of the dead at the end of time.

In confirmation we reaffirm the promises which were made at our baptism, and we are given strength through the Spirit to live the new life we have been given in baptism, and protection from all that would turn us away from God.

The Church of England's normative confirmation service, to which the Common Worship services are authorised alternatives, is the confirmation service in the 1662 Book of Common Prayer.

This little book provides an introduction to the 1662 service. It describes how confirmation developed in the Early Church and during the Middle Ages and how the Prayer Book confirmation service developed after the Reformation. It also provides a detailed commentary on the Prayer Book service, and answers the ten key questions people today generally ask about confirmation.

Milton Keynes UK
Ingram Content Group UK Ltd.
UKHW022131210724
445808UK00014B/59

9 781906 327750